STAR WARS

A STORYBOOK BY
J.J. GARDNER

ADAPTED FROM THE SCREENPLAY BY
GEORGE LUCAS

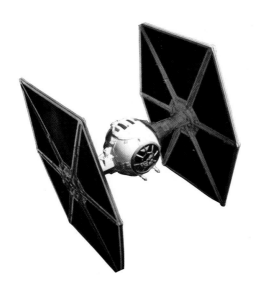

SCHOLASTIC INC.

NEW YORK   TORONTO   LONDON   AUCKLAND   SYDNEY

ISBN 0-590-06654-4

™ & ® & © 1997 by Lucasfilm Ltd. All rights reserved.
Published by Scholastic Inc.

12 11 10 9 8 7 6 5 4 3   7 8 9/9 0 1 2/0

Designed by Joan Ferrigno
Edited by Allan Kausch (Lucasfilm) and Ellen Stamper (Scholastic)

Printed in the U.S.A.   14

First Scholastic printing, February 1997

A LONG TIME AGO IN A GALAXY FAR, FAR AWAY . . . .

It is a period of civil war. Rebel spaceships, striking from a hidden base, have won their first victory against the Galactic Empire.

During the battle, Rebel spies managed to steal secret plans to the Empire's ultimate weapon, the Death Star, an armored space station with enough power to destroy an entire planet.

Pursued by the Empire's sinister agents, Princess Leia raced home aboard her starship with the stolen plans that could save her people and restore freedom to the galaxy. . . .

But the Imperial Star Destroyer, commanded by the Empire's most fearsome soldiers, including Darth Vader, overtook the Rebel ship just as it reached the nearby desert planet of Tatooine. Knowing she would soon be captured, Princess Leia hid the stolen plans in R2-D2, a droid, and ordered R2-D2 on a secret mission to the planet below.

Together with his companion robot, C-3PO, R2-D2 escaped in a small life pod while the princess was left to her fate. But no sooner had they arrived on the desert planet than the two droids were captured by Jawas, a race of scavengers who immediately made plans to sell them to the local farmers. . . .

Luke Skywalker emerged from his uncle Owen Lars' dust-covered farm hut and let out another tired sigh. He was bored. Tatooine was nothing but kilometers and kilometers of sand and dunes, a desert wasteland. And it seemed to Luke as if he might be stuck here forever.

"Luke," he heard his uncle call to him. A Jawa junk transport had stopped by the farm and his uncle had just purchased two used droids. One was very tall and the other very small. "Take these two over to the garage, will you? I want them cleaned up before dinner."

"But I was going into Toshi Station to pick up some power converters—" Luke started to reply.

"You can waste time with your friends when your chores are done," his uncle insisted. "Now come on, get to it!"

"Okay, let's go," Luke said, unhappily directing the two robots into a cluttered garage.

"This oil bath is going to feel so good!" said the tall, gold-plated droid as he lowered himself into a vat of clear slimy oil. "I've got such a bad case of dust contamination, I can barely move!"

The smaller, dome-topped droid, who was busy recharging his batteries, heartily agreed and replied with a series of satisfied electronic bleeps.

Luke, on the other hand, was becoming impatient. He had known for a long time now that he didn't want to be a moisture farmer like his Uncle Owen. Instead he wanted to be like his friend Biggs Darklighter, who had gone off to the Imperial Academy to train to be a starfighter pilot. Luke knew that he was just as good a pilot as Biggs and longed for the chance to prove it.

"It just isn't fair," Luke said aloud. "I'm never gonna get out of here."

"Is there anything I might do to help?" asked the golden droid.

"Not unless you can teleport me off this rock," replied Luke.

"I don't think so, sir," said the droid, admitting that he was powerless to do so.

"You can call me Luke."

"And I am C-3PO, human-cyborg relations," the golden droid said, introducing himself. "And this is my counterpart R2-D2."

"Hello," Luke said to the dome-headed droid. R2 responded with three cheery electronic beeps.

R2 was quite dirty so Luke began to scrape away at his connectors. Suddenly a fragment broke loose with such a snap that it sent Luke tumbling head over heels.

Without warning, R2's mechanisms began to buzz and whirr. A beam of light shot out from his little face and projected a three-dimensional image onto the floor. It was an image of a lovely but frightened woman.

"Help me, Obi-Wan Kenobi," said the projection. "You're my only hope."

"Is there more to this recording?" asked Luke with wide-eyed astonishment.

R2 replied with several frantic squeaks followed by a short, curt whistle.

"He says that he's the property of Obi-Wan Kenobi, a resident of these parts," translated C-3PO, who seemed equally astounded by the projection.

"I wonder if he means old Ben Kenobi?" Luke said, remembering an old hermit who lived beyond the rock canyons.

That evening after dinner, Luke returned to the garage only to discover that R2 had fled.

"I told him not to go," C-3PO explained frantically. "But he kept babbling on about his mission. Couldn't we go after him?"

"It's too dangerous," replied Luke. Local tribes of Sand People often attacked and robbed wanderers at night. "We'll have to wait until morning."

As soon as it was dawn, Luke revved up his sleek landspeeder. Then he and C-3PO took off across the desert in search of R2.

"Look, there's a droid on the scanner. Might be our little R2 unit," Luke said, as he piloted the landspeeder across the desert wasteland.

Sure enough it was R2, who was already halfway across the rock canyons.

"Where do you think you're going?" Luke demanded of R2 as he brought his landspeeder to a stop. But instead of answering, the little robot suddenly let out a mass of frenzied whistles and screams.

"What's wrong with him now?" Luke asked.

"He says there are several creatures approaching from the southeast," replied C-3PO.

"Sand People!" shouted Luke. He took out his electrobinoculars and peered over a ridge. R2 was right. Luke saw several banthas, the huge, fur-covered, elephant-like creatures that the Sand People used to ride through the desert.

Luke knew he had better flee or risk having his landspeeder stripped. But no sooner had he stood up to leave than a towering, robed Tusken Raider appeared through the windblown sand and pounced on him.

It was the last thing Luke saw before passing out.

When Luke awoke he saw another figure standing over him: a very old man with a cracked, weatherbeaten face and a whispy white beard. Luke recognized the man at once. It was old Ben Kenobi himself. Luke sighed with relief. Old Ben must have saved him from the clutches of the Sand People.

"You're fortunate to be all in one piece," said Ben. "Tell me, young Luke, what brings you out this far?"

"This little droid!" said Luke, pointing at R2, who had waddled over. "He claims to be the property of an Obi-Wan Kenobi. Is he a relative of yours? Do you know who he's talking about?"

A faraway look came over old Ben's dark eyes. It was as if he were remembering something from a very long time ago. "Obi-Wan Kenobi," he said to himself. "Now that's a name I've not heard in a long time."

"You know him?" asked Luke.

"Of course," said Ben, with a smile. "He's me."

Back at Ben's hut, Luke listened intently while the old man told of his days as a young Jedi Knight, of the days he and Luke's father fought side by side to keep the galaxy free. As proof of those days, Ben handed Luke a lightsaber that had once belonged to his father. Then he told of the day Luke's father died at the hands of Darth Vader, a young Jedi who became attracted to the dark side of the Force.

"The Force?" asked Luke. He had never heard of it before.

"The Force is an energy field that gives a Jedi his power," explained Ben. Then he turned to examine R2-D2. The little droid whirred and beeped until the image of the pretty woman appeared again. This time she was able to complete her message.

"General Kenobi," she said. "Years ago you served my father. I have placed information vital to the survival of the Rebellion into the memory systems of this R2 unit. My father will know how to retrieve it. You must see this droid safely to him on Alderaan. This is our most desperate hour. You're my only hope."

Ben turned to Luke. "You must learn the ways of the Force if you're to come with me to Alderaan," he said.

"I'm not going to Alderaan," laughed Luke. "I've got to get home."

"Learn about the Force, Luke," said Ben. But Luke was insistent. It wasn't that he liked the Empire. He hated it! It was just that he had responsibilities!

Luke finally agreed to take Ben as far as the city of Anchorhead. From there Ben would be able get a transport to take him on his mission to help the princess. But soon after they took off they found a Jawa sandcrawler that had been attacked. Luke recognized it as the same transport that sold R2 and C-3PO to his uncle. He realized at once that Imperial soldiers must have followed the robots to Tatooine. That meant his aunt and uncle were in great danger.

He raced home, but it was too late. The farm had been burnt to a crisp, obviously destroyed by the Imperial soldiers who were looking for R2. Luke realized the soldiers had left no survivors.

At first Luke felt scared, fearful that the Imperial soldiers were still nearby. But soon his fear turned to hatred. Hatred of the Imperial soldiers. Hatred of the Empire. As he stood among the ashen remains of what was once his home, he silently vowed to avenge the deaths of his aunt and uncle.

Now he had no choice but to go with Ben Kenobi to Anchorhead. To become a Jedi Knight like his father, and join the fight against the Empire after all.

The huge, planet-sized space station called the Death Star glided purposefully toward the planet Alderaan. Aboard it, Lord Darth Vader, second-in-command, led an Imperial torture robot away from a cell in the detention area. He had just tried to get Princess Leia to tell him the location of the hidden Rebel base, but had failed.

Frustrated and angry, he brought the princess face to face with his superior, Governor Tarkin.

"Her resistance to the mind probe is considerable," Leia heard Vader tell the governor.

"Since you are reluctant to provide us with the location of the Rebel base," Tarkin said, turning to Princess Leia. "I have chosen to test this station's destructive power on your home planet of Alderaan."

"No!" exclaimed Princess Leia. "Alderaan is peaceful. We have no weapons. You can't possibly —"

"Then name the system," demanded Tarkin. "Where is the Rebel base?"

Leia decided she had to lie if she were to save both the Rebels and the people of her homeworld. "They're on Dantooine," she replied, hoping Governor Tarkin would believe her.

"You see, Lord Vader?" The governor asked victoriously. "She can be reasonable. Continue with the operation. You may fire when ready."

"No!" Princess Leia cried out. But by then it was too late. The Death Star had blasted Alderaan into tiny bits.

Governor Tarkin, the princess realized, was ruthless.

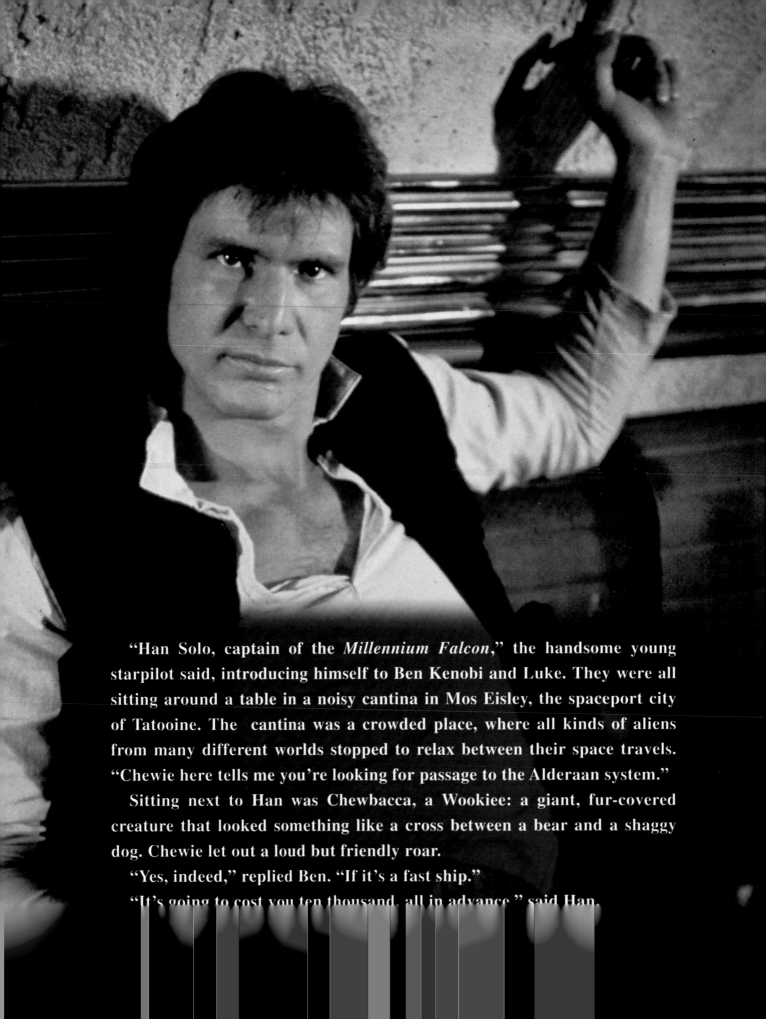

"Han Solo, captain of the *Millennium Falcon*," the handsome young starpilot said, introducing himself to Ben Kenobi and Luke. They were all sitting around a table in a noisy cantina in Mos Eisley, the spaceport city of Tatooine. The cantina was a crowded place, where all kinds of aliens from many different worlds stopped to relax between their space travels. "Chewie here tells me you're looking for passage to the Alderaan system."

Sitting next to Han was Chewbacca, a Wookiee: a giant, fur-covered creature that looked something like a cross between a bear and a shaggy dog. Chewie let out a loud but friendly roar.

"Yes, indeed," replied Ben. "If it's a fast ship."

"It's going to cost you ten thousand, all in advance," said Han.

"Ten thousand!" exclaimed Luke, shocked at the high price. "We could almost buy our own ship for that!"

"But who's going to fly it, kid?" asked Han with a smirk. "You?"

"You bet I could," insisted Luke. "I'm not such a bad pilot myself."

In spite of Luke's objections, Ben Kenobi agreed to pay Han enough money to help them reach Alderaan.

Han and Chewbacca hastened to Docking Bay 94. In the center of the large hangar was Han's spaceship, the *Millennium Falcon*. Standing in front of the ship was a thick, hulking creature that looked like a cross between a giant earthworm and a living mudpile.

Han recognized the creature as Jabba the Hutt. Jabba was a notorious crimelord and Han owed him a lot of money.

"I've been waiting for you," said Han. "You didn't think I was gonna run did you?"

"Why haven't you paid me?" Jabba asked Han.

"I got a nice easy charter now," Han replied. He and Chewbacca cautiously walked around the slow-moving creature. As they did so Han deliberately stepped on the big worm's tail, causing Jabba's eyes to momentarily bug out. "I'll pay you back plus a little extra."

Jabba agreed, but added: "If you fail me again I'll put a price on your head so big you won't be able to go near a civilized system."

"Jabba, you're a wonderful human being," Han said with a smirk. Then he and Chewbacca climbed the ramp and boarded the *Millennium Falcon*.

Han and Chewbacca were busy making final lift-off adjustments on the *Millennium Falcon* when Luke, Ben, and the droids arrived at Docking Bay 94.

"What a piece of junk!" exclaimed Luke once he saw the large, round, beat-up hunk of a spaceship.

"She may not look like much, but she's got it where it counts, kid," insisted Han. "I've made a lot of special modifications myself."

Luke scratched his head. As he boarded the *Falcon* he was becoming uncertain they would ever get to Alderaan at all.

Just then a commotion started in the docking bay. Luke spun around and looked through the ship's viewport. Seven Imperial stormtroopers had just made their way inside.

"Stop that ship!" commanded one of the troopers. "Blast them!"

But before the troopers could get off a shot Han drew his laser pistol and popped off a couple of blasts at them. The troopers dived for safety. That gave Han just enough time to climb unharmed into the cockpit of the *Falcon*.

"Chewie, get us out of here!" he commanded his Wookiee co-pilot as he strapped himself in. Within seconds, Chewbacca set the controls and the *Falcon* blasted off into space.

"Oh, my," groaned C-3PO as the ship left Tatooine's orbit. "I'd forgotten how much I hate space travel."

But the danger wasn't over yet. Luke and the others could see that they were being followed by two huge Imperial Star Destroyers.

"Why don't you outrun them?" Luke asked Han. "I thought you said this thing was fast."

"We'll be safe enough once we make the jump to hyperspace," replied Han, as he set the controls that would take the *Falcon* light years beyond the reach of the Star Destroyers. "Here's where the fun begins!"

Just then a laser blast from one of the Star Destroyers violently rocked the ship from side to side. Then came another blast, and another, and another.

"Go strap yourself in!" Han ordered. "I'm going to make the jump to lightspeed." Then he quickly pressed a series of switches. The *Falcon* shook for a moment. The galaxy brightened. Suddenly the ship took off at an incredible speed, leaving the Imperial Star Destroyers far behind.

When Han saw that they were approaching Alderaan, he knew it was time to bring the ship out of hyperspace. But no sooner had the ship returned to normal speed than it was bombarded by a meteor shower!

"What's going on?" asked Luke.

"Our position is correct," replied Han. "Except — no Alderaan."

They were stunned. Somehow the planet of Alderaan had been completely destroyed. It was nothing now but a mass of hurtling meteorites.

"Destroyed by the Empire!" exclaimed Ben.

"The entire starfleet couldn't destroy the whole planet," said Han. "It would take a thousand ships with more fire power than I've —"

But before Han could finish his sentence a muffled alarm started to hum over the loudspeaker. The *Falcon*'s radar had picked up another Imperial fighter ship. Only this time it passed right by the *Falcon* and then continued into deep space.

"If they identify us, we're in big trouble," warned Luke.

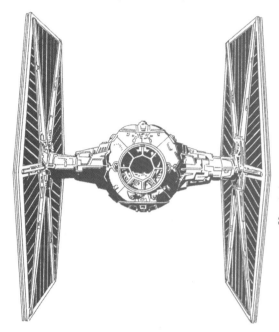

"Well, he ain't going to be around long enough to tell anybody about us," said Han. And with that he set the *Falcon* after the ship.

The *Falcon* followed the Imperial fighter as it headed toward a small moon. As the *Falcon* got closer, however, the crew realized the object wasn't a moon at all, but a huge space station as large as a small planet. It was the biggest space station anyone had ever seen.

"Turn the ship around!" shouted Ben. The space station was the Empire's dreadful Death Star, a weapon capable of destroying entire planets.

But Han and Chewbacca were unable to reverse the ship. The tiny *Millennium Falcon* was no match for a powerful tractor beam that was now pulling them into the Death Star itself. In a matter of moments, the *Falcon* had been drawn inside the great space station and was being lowered onto the floor of a huge hangar.

The *Falcon* was then flooded with a search team of white-armored Imperial soldiers. The soldiers searched the *Falcon* from top to bottom, but found it completely deserted. No sooner had they left the ship than two floor panels popped up. Han, Chewbacca, Ben, and Luke had hidden beneath the *Falcon*'s floor for safety.

But Han knew they were still trapped. "Even if I could take off, I'd never get past the tractor beam," he said.

"Leave that to me," said Ben Kenobi. He had a plan. First Han and Luke disguised themselves as Imperial stormtroopers. Then, together with Chewbacca and the droids, they searched the Death Star until they discovered a computer outlet. With the help of R2-D2, they soon knew exactly where the main power controls for the tractor beam were.

"A power loss will release the *Falcon* and allow us to leave," C-3PO pointed out.

"I must go alone," said Ben.

"I want to go with you," said Luke, fearing for the old man's safety.

"You must deliver the droids safely or other star systems will suffer the same fate as Alderaan," Ben explained. "Your destiny lies along a different path from mine. The Force will be with you always!"

And with that Ben Kenobi adjusted his lightsaber and took off down the long gray hallway.

Just then R2 let out a series of frantic bleeps. The little droid sounded as if he were in a panic.

"He says 'I found her.' " translated C-3PO. " 'She's here.' "

"Who has he found?" asked Luke.

"Princess Leia," replied C-3PO. "She's scheduled to be terminated."

"We've got to do something," said Luke. "We've got to help her."

Han protested. He had been paid for one thing only: to bring Luke, Ben, and the droids to Alderaan. Besides, he had gotten himself in enough trouble so far. Right now all he wanted was for Ben to turn off the tractor beam so he could escape in one piece.

"But if you were to rescue the princess the reward would be more wealth than you could imagine," said Luke, knowing that Han needed money.

Han realized he had no choice. He decided to help Luke. Posing as stormtroopers, the two pretended that Chewbacca was their prisoner and walked safely through the halls of the Death Star until they reached the detention security area. Once there, Han and Chewie had to blast their way past several guards, while Luke raced ahead to one of the holding cells.

Inside the cell, resting on a cot, was Princess Leia. Luke had only seen her in the projected message she had sent to Ben Kenobi. Now, seeing her in real life, he was momentarily startled by her beauty.

"Aren't you a little short for a stormtrooper?" the princess asked.

"I'm Luke Skywalker," replied Luke. "I'm here to rescue you. I'm here with Ben Kenobi."

"Ben Kenobi!" Princess Leia exclaimed happily. "Where is he?"

"Come on!" beckoned Luke. Then he led the princess out of the detention cell.

"Obi-Wan Kenobi is here," Darth Vader said to Governor Tarkin as they stood in the conference room of the Death Star. "There was a tremor in the Force. The last time I felt it was in the presence of my old master."

"Surely he must be dead by now," said the governor. "The Jedi are extinct, their fire has gone out of the universe."

"Don't underestimate the Force," said Vader.

Just then a quiet alarm buzzed over the intercom. Word of Princess Leia's escape was coming through.

But Vader wasn't concerned with Princess Leia now. "Obi-Wan is here," he said. "The Force is with him."

"If you're right, he must not be allowed to escape," said the governor.

"Escape is not his plan," said Vader. "I must face him alone."

And with that Darth Vader took off to search for his old master.

Princess Leia followed Luke, Han, and Chewbacca into the detention area. Imperial stormtroopers were all around now, shooting at them along the corridors of the Death Star.

"Can't get out this way!" shouted Han as they were faced with more troopers.

"Looks like you managed to cut off our only escape route," Princess Leia said to Han.

"Maybe you'd like it back in your cell, Your Highness," Han replied sharply as he aimed his gun and blasted at the stormtroopers ahead.

"This is some rescue," the princess quipped as she dodged a return blast from one of the troopers. "When you came in here, didn't you have a plan for getting out?"

Before Han could answer, Princess Leia took Luke's pistol and blasted a hole through a small grate in the wall beside them.

"What are you doing?" Han asked.

"Somebody has to save our skins," said the princess. "Into the garbage chute, fly boy."

Quickly Han and Luke followed Princess Leia through the hole and down a long, twisting chute. One by one they landed in a dark, cavernous room filled with slimy, murky, smelly galactic garbage.

"What an incredible smell you discovered!" Han taunted Princess Leia. "Let's get out of here!"

Han aimed his laser pistol at a door and fired. But instead of blasting through the door, his laser beam bounced wildly around the room. The garbage chamber was magnetically sealed!

Just then a loud, horrible, inhuman moan worked its way up from the murky depths of the garbage.

"There's something alive in here!" exclaimed Luke. No sooner had he said it than an oozy tentacle reached up and yanked him down into the muck.

"Blast it!" Luke shouted to Han. "My gun's jammed!"

Han aimed his pistol and fired downward at the ugly tentacle, but missed. He aimed again, but now the tentacle pulled Luke down a second time.

Then . . . nothing.

For a moment Han, Leia, and Chewbacca were deathly silent. It looked as if Luke was gone forever. Then, without warning, the room began to rumble and they were nearly thrown off their feet. The walls of the giant compactor were moving, closing in on them. In a moment they would be crushed to death!

Suddenly something bobbed up from the muck below. It was Luke, gasping for air. The strange, tentacled creature, obviously frightened by the rumbling walls, had freed him.

Seeing the walls were closing in, Luke thought fast. He called C-3PO and R2 on his communicator. "Shut down all the garbage mashers on the detention level!" he ordered the droids, who were still linked up to the Death Star's computer system.

Luke and the others waited breathlessly. Seconds seemed like minutes. Then, with the walls only precious centimeters away from turning them into crushed rubbish, the garbage masher came to a grinding stop. R2 had done it!

"Now open the maintenance hatch," Luke ordered R2. No sooner had he given the order than the maintenance hatch popped open. Everyone filed safely out. Then they headed toward the main hangar and the *Millennium Falcon*.

Darth Vader hurried along the halls of the Death Star toward the main hangar. He knew that he would probably find Obi-Wan trying to flee to the *Millennium Falcon*.

He was correct. When he reached the hallway that led to the main hangar, he stopped and waited. Before long, Ben came running around the corner.

"I've been waiting for you, Obi-Wan," said Vader. "When I left you I was but the learner. Now I am the master."

"Only a master of evil, Darth," said Ben. At that Vader pulled out his lightsaber and ignited it. Ben did the same with his. Then the two powerful Jedis lunged at each other, locking their swords in battle.

At that moment another door to the hangar opened. In rushed Luke and the others.

"Now's our chance," said Han, when he saw that the Imperial troopers who had been guarding the *Falcon* had sped to the aide of Darth Vader. "Go!"

But upon seeing that Ben was in danger, Luke stopped. He reached for his lightsaber, but he was unable to help. Darth Vader had just sliced his sword right through old Ben Kenobi.

"No!" cried Luke. Anger and hatred for Darth Vader welled up inside him.

"Come on," Princess Leia called. But Luke couldn't move. "Luke, it's too late."

She's right, thought Luke as he reluctantly joined his friends. Ben Kenobi had vanished right before his eyes.

The *Millennium Falcon* blasted off safely from the Death Star and headed for the Rebel base on Yavin Four, a moon of the planet Yavin.

"Not a bad bit of rescuing, huh?" Han asked proudly. "You know sometimes I even amaze myself."

"That doesn't sound too hard," teased Princess Leia. "They let us go. It's the only explanation."

Everyone knew that Leia was right. No sooner had they landed on Yavin Four than word came that the Death Star was approaching them.

Princess Leia quickly had the secret plans removed from R2's computer banks and gave them to the Rebel commander. After looking at the plans, the Rebels learned that there was only one way they could destroy the Death Star: by sending a ship right up a channel at its middle and dropping a torpedo down its thermal exhaust port. It was a mission that required pinpoint accuracy.

Luke donned a starfighter pilot's uniform. He was going to help the Rebel pilots destroy the Death Star. As he prepared to board an X-wing starfighter he noticed that Han had collected his reward and was getting ready to go.

"So, you got your reward and you're just leaving?" asked Luke, angry and disappointed. He had hoped that Han would stay and join the Rebels in their fight against the Empire.

"What good's a reward if you ain't around to use it," Han replied, selfishly. "Besides, attacking the battle station ain't my idea of courage. It's more like suicide."

And with that Luke and Han said their good-byes.

Luke climbed into the cockpit of his starfighter and strapped on his helmet.

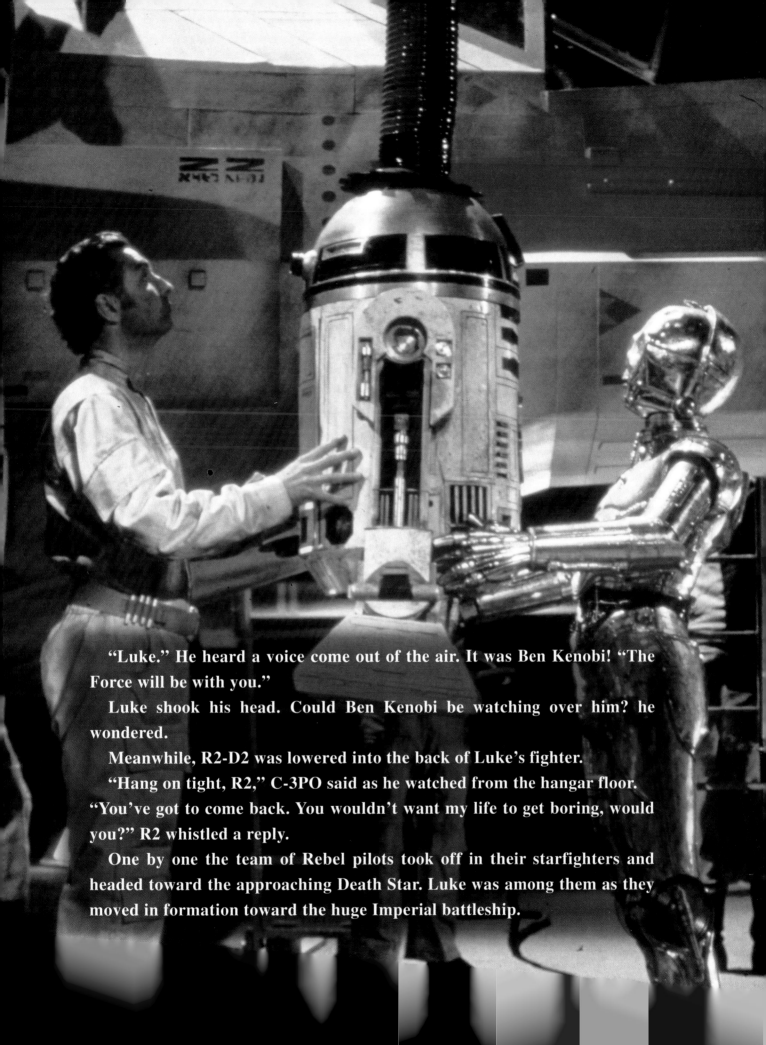

"Luke." He heard a voice come out of the air. It was Ben Kenobi! "The Force will be with you."

Luke shook his head. Could Ben Kenobi be watching over him? he wondered.

Meanwhile, R2-D2 was lowered into the back of Luke's fighter.

"Hang on tight, R2," C-3PO said as he watched from the hangar floor. "You've got to come back. You wouldn't want my life to get boring, would you?" R2 whistled a reply.

One by one the team of Rebel pilots took off in their starfighters and headed toward the approaching Death Star. Luke was among them as they moved in formation toward the huge Imperial battleship.

"Look at the size of that thing!" exclaimed one of the pilots as he made his approach.

Immediately the Rebels headed up the channel at the center of the Death Star and zeroed in on its thermal exhaust port. But before long a team of Imperial TIE fighters was on their trail.

"Watch your back, Luke!" one of the pilots warned.

Luke looked up to see a TIE fighter closing in on him fast. The TIE sent a laser blast at Luke's ship, setting one of its wings on fire.

"I'm hit, but not bad!" exclaimed Luke. Then, as R2 made the necessary repairs, Luke spun his fighter back into formation.

By then the Death Star was surrounded in a blaze of galactic warfare. Lasers blasted everywhere. TIE fighters and Rebel fighters fought viciously. Many were destroyed on either side.

Luke was now at the front of the Rebel formation and was heading straight for the thermal exhaust port. The other fighters covered him, fighting off TIE ships so that Luke could drop his torpedoes and destroy the Death Star. But the power of the Imperial fighters was too great for the Rebels. One by one they were destroyed.

Suddenly Luke was completely alone. And right behind him, closing fast, was the TIE fighter piloted by Darth Vader himself.

Luke tensed as he charged toward the thermal exhaust port. He was trying his best to line up the cross-hairs on his ship's targeting screen. If he was so much as a fraction off, then the mission would be lost and the Death Star would destroy the Rebel base.

"Use the Force, Luke," he suddenly heard the voice of Ben Kenobi call to him. "Let go."

Luke was momentarily startled at the sound of Ben's voice. Back on the *Millennium Falcon*, Ben had showed Luke how to use the Force to fight with a lightsaber. All Luke had to do was close his eyes and rely on the Force to guide him. Now Ben was telling him to do the same thing.

"Luke." He heard Ben again. "Trust me."

Luke reached down and turned off his targeting computer. Then he looked anxiously through his viewport until he caught sight of the Death Star's exhaust port and barreled toward it.

Behind him Darth Vader was coming on fast.

"I have you now," Vader said to himself as he targeted Luke's ship.

Just then a laser blast came from out of nowhere, hitting one of the two TIE fighters that were flanking Vader. The fighter crashed into Vader's ship, sending the ship spinning out of control and deep into outer space.

Luke glanced around. The *Millennium Falcon* had come to his rescue!

"Yahoo!" Luke heard a voice yell over his intercom. It was Han Solo! "You're all clear, kid. Now let's blow this thing and go home!"

Luke looked up and smiled. Then he closed his eyes and let the Force help him concentrate on the thermal exhaust port. When he was sure he was ready, he pressed a button and fired his torpedoes.

It was a direct hit! Luke veered his starfighter up and away from the Death Star just as the space station exploded in a huge yellow fireball.

"Great shot, kid!" exclaimed Han over the intercom. "That was one in a million!"

When Luke and Han returned to the Rebel base they were greeted with cheers from everybody. Princess Leia placed special golden medals of valor around their necks. Chewbacca growled with pride. C-3PO stood proudly on the side and watched. And R2-D2 beeped with happiness.

Luke beamed with pride. He had faced many dangers since he left Tatooine. Together with his new friends he had fought many battles. He was a Rebel fighter now and had the medal to prove it.

Nevertheless an uneasy feeling overcame Luke as he looked at the ceremony going on around him. The Death Star may have been destroyed, but the Emperor was still alive.

Deep down, he knew that the war was not over. In fact, it was just beginning.

TO BE CONTINUED . . .